MW00909848

Spirit to Spirit

A Collection of Poetry, Meditations
and
Soul Verse

by

Leigh Karen Graves-Ware, D.Min., MSW

Spirit to Spirit
A Collection of Poetry, Meditations
and Soul Verse

Copyright © 2008
Leigh Karen Graves-Ware

Publisher:
Leigh Karen Graves-Ware
P.O. Box 136 Waterford 06385

CONTENTS

Acknowledgements

To my mother who carried me and nurtured me; It was you and me against the world.

To my dad who came to my rescue right before it was too late and spoke destiny and hope into my being; Good Stock.

To my husband, the lover of my soul; Love melodies forever.

To my daughter, Chloe; Your brilliance and potential dazzles like rubies.

To my son, Malvin; You can accomplish anything because of the depth of God's love in your heart.

To my mentors, teachers, coaches, friends, supervisors, co-workers and enemies; I would like to say "thank you".

Because of you this book has been written.

Thank You to Pastors

To my spiritual parents, Rev. Johnny L. Burns, Sr. and Rev. Sharon L. Burns: What would I have done without you... Thank you for teaching me the Word that gives me the words to express myself. It is an honor and a privilege to be connected to you and the New Life family.

Section One
Poetic Voice - Personal Process

Who Am I? - A Woman of Purpose

 Woman of Purpose. God has given me Peace
to quiet the turmoil and chaos I found inside.
He has given me Peace to hush the silent cries and wipe away the tears.
This is all part of the process.
My process to be what He is fashioning. A masterpiece. A work of art.

Could the clay dare to speak out in disdain at the Potter and His creation?
Not so.
The clay has no input into what it will be made like, and what it's function will be.
It must submit to the kneading and shaping of the Potter's Hand.

I am tried by the fire of my experience and
molded by the Hand of the Master.

Pure Gold. A Diamond from the pressure all
around me.

The fire and the pressure is nothing but the
circumstances,

issues, and uncertainties of life.

The heat and pressure almost seems
unbearable, but necessary to make me.

Oh Clay what do you have to say? Nothing but
Yes.

The response of yieldedness and submission -
is my Yes Lord.

He will make it all work for my good. The
praise of His Glory.

What I am. What I shall be. His workmanship.
Made in His image.

Smoothing out the rough edges and making me
beautiful.

Beauty for ashes - exchanging pain and past for
purpose, recycling.

I'm being made into a vessel of honor, fit for
the Master's use.
One day, I'll be put on display for all to see,
and some will wonder how I came to be.
I will tell them about the process.
Uncomfortable it my seem.
It will be worth it all just to be exactly what He
called and envisioned me to be.

The Dance

he dance is a story of interaction with my environment.
It was hostile at times.
An orchestrated dance with friends and foes.

Step to the music.
The sounds of truth in chorus marching with the beat of time.
Time.
Standing on righteousness, yet dancing with courage and patience.

The process.
Stretching, changing, growing.

Step by step approach to destiny.
My moment.

At my right hand is purpose; at my left hand is grace.
Peace at my feet and thy Word in my mouth.

Movement. Exchange. Giving up the old for the new.

An encounter.
I serenade my present and waltz with my future.
The Holy Spirit is my partner on the dance floor of adversity.
History is in the making.

Transition - From what I was.
I see Glory.
I see Destiny Fulfilled.
I am what He promised.

The dance brought me to be.

When He Loved Me

Man that I love, set a place for me.
Loved me regardless of how I responded.

Loved me when I didn't love myself.
Loved me when I could do nothing but cry and mourn.
Loved me when I was lost and confused.
Loved me even though I had been abused and misused.
Loved me despite my anger and insecurity.
Loved me although I was afraid.
Loved me regardless of how I looked or what I said.

Loved me instead of leaving me.
Loved me instead of mistreating me.

Didn't know it was possible to love me that way.

Loved me and lead me.
Loved me and helped me.
Loved me and encouraged me.
Loved me and supported me.
Loved me and upheld me.
Loved me and put me before you.
Loved me and prayed for me.
Loved me and stayed with me.

Loved me and Loved me and Loved me and Loved me.

Exemplified the Father's Love when you loved me.

Written for Malvin

Reclaim Your Voice

 eclaim your voice oh woman.

Woman of God.

Take your place in God's Army. Get up from where you've stumbled and fallen. It's okay, He'll restore you. He's prepared a place for you in His army. He's prepared a place for you to lead in battle. You have to take your position of authority. You have to take your place and reclaim your space in the Spirit. Open wide your mouth and Declare His Glory! Shout His

Promises! Open wide your Mouth oh woman of Praise! Only you can fulfill the destiny He's designed for you. Open wide your mouth and sing! Sing of His Glory! Sing and Declare His Word! We need to hear your voice – mother. If you don't reclaim it? Who will teach the young women? Who will train your daughters oh woman of Zion. Who will do it?

Oh woman of Prayer. Mighty in battle. Intercession and travail, you must bring forth the promise. You were created precisely for this purpose Oh woman. You can do it.

Join in oneness with the man of God. Your covering. Your Boaz. Walk in God's order and submit in obedience to His Authority. Mighty man of God, Mighty woman of God, together, as one, that is the promise, the call, the fulfillment of destiny. You shall bring forth. You shall manifest His Glory in the earth. You shall complete to work that has been placed at your charge. Oh Mighty woman of God. Reclaim your voice. Reclaim your voice. Don't wait any longer, reclaim your voice.

Mighty Warrior - Mighty Man

Mighty Warrior awake and arise from your slumber. Have you forgotten? Don't you know that you are strong and courageous? Put off sleep, put away rest and take up your sword and your shield. Get dressed for battle. Prepare and arm yourself.

Haven't you noticed the onslaught of the enemy? He has tried to capture your attention with worries and cares, problems and pressures. To distract you all the while sifting you like wheat. His plan was to steal your anointing. To steal your seed, the Word of God. To make you helpless.

Wake up oh sleeper! Stand at attention. Arise mighty man of valor to slay the bear and the lion. Get ready to take instructions from the King. His strategies and plans will not fail. He is the Lord. Take your place oh Mighty Man. You are a covering and leader and servant all at the same time. Like the example of Jesus you have a backbone of iron and a face of flint Oh strong man. You are anointed for service.

Minister to the Lord and obey Him. You are

strong yet gentle, proud yet humble. Meek.

Fierce yet compassionate.

You are the mighty man leading by example.

We will follow you as you follow Christ. Set

the pace and run the race, Oh Mighty Man.

Enter into battle and tear down the strongholds

of the enemy. Declare with your mouth the

victory of the Lord. He goes before you and He

is your rear guard.

Wake up Oh Mighty Man of Valor! Arise and take up your armor and your sword. Don't you see the attack of the enemy? Get dressed for battle, ready yourself for the fight.

Aren't you tired of the enemy getting the best of you? Don't you hear him laughing while you lay down in your circumstances?

He comes to steal, kill and destroy the relationship you have with your wife, kill your children and rob you of your productivity for the kingdom.

\\

Don't you see the patterns? The open doors?

Your father, his father, and his father. All had

the same problem? You wake up one day and

find yourself going down the same road? But

you don't want to… How did you get here? Is

this the gift you'll leave for your son too?

Break the curse and chains that hold you. It's a

spiritual thing. Close the doors and cut the ties.

Did you know that God called you to be a

mighty man of valor. Strong. Courageous.

If one could get free and stay free. Take your

place…get in line

Superhero

How Much does it cost for one man to be My Superhero? A cape and a suit and answers to my questions. How much is it worth to step into shoes you didn't choose and become just what I needed at the right time?

You are a legend. An archetype. The one and only.

\\

Time seems to have stopped.

You live in my memories.

Never forgotten is too trivial to describe you.

Powerful and dependable, you are My

Superhero.

You taught me how to lead, taught me how to

find solutions to questions. You taught me how

to be 10 steps ahead, even when all thought I

was 10 steps behind. You taught me color

didn't matter – even though yours sometime

brought closed doors. You showed me how to

\\\

push past pain to pave the way for those following me. You taught me love was a two way street and trust was earned. You showed me how to be a champion in a game where you could have easily been a quitter or a failure. You taught me how to gain, even when much had been lost, then only to give it away.

Learning by watching was my best school.

\\

How much did it cost you to become daddy to a child you never knew? Seeds planted now show your love harvest. The legacy left is far greater than the time invested because it keeps reproducing. Live never ends but multiplies. Thank you My Superhero, Maybe soon I'll grow up to be just like you.

Written in Memory of

Melvin Laverne Davis 8-9-06

\\

Rock A Bye

Children who are drunk with pleasure, fattened by indulgence and enjoyment. The enemy's lullabye....................Gently rocking her to sleep.

Although she is pregnant with vision,

eventhough he is full of purpose.

Ever so gently, falling

Falling,

Falling asleep.

Rock a bye of the enemy.

The Father sends a warning

Wake Up Oh Slumberer!

My child arise from your sleep and enter into

my presence

Arise and make ready for battle!

Dress in Your Holy Armour!

Warring daughter and Warring Son

Take your place and man your post

Take up your Sword and your Shield.

My Word in your Mouth and Shout!

March in step with My Spirit. Keep Up! Keep

Pace!

Child stay in line.

Oh Son, Oh Daughter

There Is Ground to Gain and Little Time.

Come To The Table

"He prepares a table for me in the presence

of mine enemies" Psalm 23:8

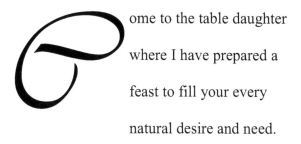ome to the table daughter
where I have prepared a
feast to fill your every
natural desire and need.

In comfort be seated, you will be served and
well treated.

At my table I have established beforehand a place for you to rest and be filled with my glory and my presence.

Something happened when I came to the table. It was well prepared in advance for me to sit and dine with my King.

The menu was selected by Divine choice and the guest list completed without a second thought. The King invited all of my acquaintances that have been there during my making and molding process. The Chief Potter left out none of them who were like sandpaper, intense heat pressure and heat they were towards me. He said "Come to the table" they arrived an waited patiently for the event to begin.

I had no idea, I didn't realize in my coming was how I would win.

There is something to be said about obedience to the Master's Command. He said "Come to the table my daughter" so I made my way without haste to His throne. On this table were many choice delicacies and splendor arrayed, but most of all my enemies were all displayed. And so I sat at the table He prepared with my enemies all around – In His peace and rest I found.

There is a process of coming to the table: obedience, sacrifice, faith and trust with each step, God's will for my life I accepted. But most of all transition occurred just when I arrived and sat in my seat. To rest and eat in His presence among enemies and not be ensnared? I am not afraid of them, for they are like lions with no teeth.

A new place in God is where I went to the day I obeyed and sat down at the table; my agenda down I laid. The table is a place of rest, filling, eating fellowship, intimacy, sharing receiving; Impartation, digestion, transition, blessing, restoration; Increase, promise, fulfillment, my appointment with destiny.

What did I bring with me when I came to the table?

Hunger, emptiness, thirst; My spiritual need. A humble heart to realize God Himself could satisfy me. A surrendered heart and mind; the posture to receive. An obedient spirit to the Word of God that called me. My needs, my hopes to fulfill purpose.

My desires and dreams; God given. Petitions, prayers, requests sent out. My openness to hear and be lead. Patience and willingness to sit as long as it takes to receive. Jesus also came to the table. It was a place of transition for Him; An appointment with destiny to give His life for humanity.

My brother, my sister have I but one more thing;

Have you found your seat at the Master's table for which God prepared for thee?

\\

A Damascus Road experience she shall have while on her way pursuing truth; Seeking her own agenda, an experience with Jesus occurred.

The Holy Spirit; The Man of Fire appeared suddenly and they fell down as dead men; Unable to stand. Doctrines falling down in the face of God's Truth.

Seeking truth? He Is The Truth. The Spirit of Truth appeared, and Saul met Jesus on that road; He was never the same again. One experience with God's Presence and His Truth Permanently Changed him.

The course of his life altered. The plan of the devil faltered. The Truth was made known and revelation manifested in his heart.

The Power of God plus The Truth equals Revelation

Jesus..Equals..Word..Equals..Truth

Permanent Change; True Purpose Revealed.

\\\

~

The Damascus Road – Didn't realize was

where I walked to pursue my own agenda,

trying to explain and understand the Truth. But

on the road, was I introduced to Jesus, my

Salvation; Truth in Power and Demonstration.

Completely Changed; My mind re-arranged.

My purpose pure, understanding sure. No

Doubt; I believe! My life Re-Ordered, the

devil's plan for me cancelled.

Saula to Paula; Never the same; On the

Damascus Road I was changed.

\\\

Truth I now receive. Understand. I heard His command.

Calling My Name, I was freed; From the pursuit of so many things. In pursuit now of His Presence; Revealed to Me is the reason for my existence.

No More

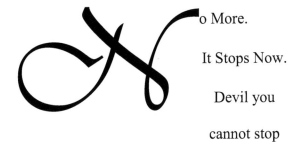o More.

It Stops Now.

Devil you

cannot stop

me.

God's Not forgotten me.

I will go forth and reach destiny.

No more fear.

No more stumbling.

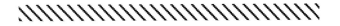

Can't Stop me. Can't Stop me. Can't Stop me.

Can't Stop me.

Submitted to God.

Resisting your tactics.

Flee from me.

You can't stop me.

I will Be.

For My Child

other Now

I am.

Much to

give;

Learning to understand.

Release the gift unobstructed. Life's language;

Love.

For my daughter, Chloe; You are so special it's

indescribable. China eyes from your nana,

chocolate cream frame and hair silky black.

You Are my child of promise.

My first born, to be me and daddy; Breathing
and achieving. You glorify God with your life,
each step; Each choice you make. Beautiful
daughter – Mighty in the Spirit. God has Big
plans for you. Not for later, but starting now.
Your mind He crafted and designed. Sing His
praises and Live! For Jesus you will be great
along the way.

For my son, Malvin; You are honorable and
dear. Round deep caffe eyes, frame built from

your daddy and Great Grandfather Greenleaf,

Hair curly and wavy.

You Are my child of strength.

Came as baby boy, within you run sensitive and

deep waters; Mommy and daddy wrapped up

together. You bring God pleasure with your life

as you love and Obey – Fulfill the call on your

name. Make God happy; Do what He says.

Beautiful son – Mighty in grace; God's plans

for you are Great! Not to be overlooked,

starting now. Play for God's glory. For Him

only Live! Speak about Jesus, He will bless you

and keep you always.

Untitled

 walked past the gate towards the fire. It was there from things lost that I laid down my pain At the altar of sacrifice. The place to lay down what was held behind locked doors in the recesses of my mind.

The doorknob was on my side all this time.

I never realized there were hindrances to my

worship.

Paralyzing pain, unrealized anger, frustration,

rejection, forgotten distractions,

habits; A chain reaction.

To the Holy Place I am going, Yet I must

remain a moment Still - The fire burning at the

Brazen Altar of sacrifice. My flesh dying,

things burning So I can enter in. A Consuming

Fire Is the Holy Spirit. A Purifying Fire – The

Refiner, Removing the dross so the Gold can

be revealed.

Burn It Up Lord! Everything that's not like you

So I can see You in me, Dead to flesh Alive to

thee.

Willing to lay down my desires To take Your

plan for me

Fulfilling Your Purpose In the Holy Place I'll

Be.

\\\

Black

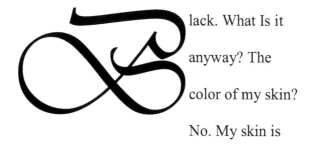lack. What Is it anyway? The color of my skin? No. My skin is creamy brown and my hair is wavy.

A Black man? A White man? Check the box.

Which one are you? What percentage makes

me Black? Is it who I identify with? My

history? My heritage? African. American

Indian. Cape Verdean. And yes, White too. I

am all of these. Great stories in my history. Yet not enough to make me free.

From Kings and Queens – Ancient Civilizations, The land of Cush, Egypt, Ethiopia, Lybia – It's in the Word of God.

"Remember Your History!" are the words I hear loud and clear. Yes! I'll remember, I'll look back in the past of ancestors last. But today I will teach my babies to reach . Reach out to Heaven to a God who can hear your questions and give you answers. Give you truth. Give you balance. Only the truth can make us free. The truth is the Word from God

the Father. Jesus is the Truth. He came and

broke the slavery bonds from days past,

provided a way of escape then and now.

Black is a color. Devoid of hue. I am the

Master's Child, skillfully and wonderfully

made. You can't squeeze me into a box.

There's just too much I won't fit.

Perspective. I remember, but I press. I press

toward the mark of the High call in Christ

Jesus. Knowing who I am and whose I am.

Knowing if I'm not careful, the past will repeat

itself. Knowing I must forgive to live. 70 times 7. Knowing that there is neither Jew nor Greek, Bond nor Free, We are One.

One God, One Word, One Faith, One Spirit, One Baptism, One Lord, One Body going to heaven. I won't be living in the projects in the Black section in heaven.

There is a great big heaven for a body who has become One with Christ as the head. To get there I must love you and you must love me, regardless of the past. Love covers a multitude of sin, that is how we will become one. Not a

Black or White or Latino or American Indian

Body of Christ. But the Body, fitly joined

together with no ism, schism, division or

respecter of person. Together we are going, so

together we must live.

Don't call me Black call me free.

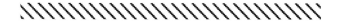

Mother's Gift

A gift for mother is what I bring today. It's not an expensive bracelet or a pretty nightgown or even a new watch. The gift that I have to bring to mother today is only my life and a few words to say. The words are thank you mom for carrying me and bringing me forth. Thank you for nursing me and nourishing me when I needed a gentle touch and an encouraging word. Thank you for tucking me into bed at night and reading my favorite storybook. Thank you for rocking me to sleep when I was afraid and letting me keep the lights on all night. Thank you for teaching me how to rollerskate and ride a bike, and even picking me up when I fell down and skinned my knees. Thank you for teaching me right from wrong and telling me about the birds and the bees. I could go on and on telling you thank you for so many things, but most of all I want to say I love you for the love you bring.

Today, a gift for mother, I bring all the things you taught me, the cherished memories, and the love of God in my heart that makes me sing. I bring my life, the choice I made to live for Jesus and through my life bring Glory to His Name. I bring my life reaching out to help others learn and grow, somehow as I reach, you reach, because I am a part of you. The blood that runs through my veins was once yours too. I recognize as each day passes, how much more I grow to be like you were years ago. In many ways we are different, yet much the same.

A gift for mother today I bring my life to worship God and serve Him on display. The Bible teaches that I must honor and heed to teaching of my mother. A Gift for mother I bring honor, respect, love and forgiveness today. The gift I also bring to the mothers that have also nurtured me along the way, thank you for the seeds you planted in me. They will eventually grow into a great harvest, and blessings you will reap from God one day. A gift for mother, today; I'll remember to say I love you and God loves you too on this special day.

\\

The Black 'Thang'

o you believe the dream? Did you hear the dreamer? We must recognize that the dreamer got the dream from a source greater than himself. The dream is for the Black child and the White child and the Yellow child and the Red child. It came from God. Unity. We are no different in God's eyes. We are His creation, all in need of a Savior.

\\\

Black Rage. White Confusion. Indifference.
Pain. Anger. Resentment. Blame. The enemy
has one man hating another because of the
color. But Jesus came that we might have life
and have it more abundantly.

Who am I? I am blood bought, , blood washed,
God sees me red – Covered by His Blood.

History! Know your history! Know your roots!
Remember where you came from. Remember
the shackles, the chains, the whip of the master.
Remember the struggles of your past.

Yes. Yes remember. Oh but you must forgive.
You must let go to obtain true liberty.
Recognize It was not the *man* who oppressed
you. It was not the man who oppressed you. It
was not the *man* who stole you from the
motherland. The thief comes, but to steal, kill
and destroy. But it is Jesus Christ that has come
to give you Life. Liberty. To release you from
your prison.

Prison is your Us Vs. Them mentality. Prison is
your unrelenting pursuit for knowledge because
someone once told you knowledge is power,
and you could not have it. Prison is the cancer

that eats alive inside because you won't
forgive. Hatred. Prejudice. Where is the Love
of God?

To be free, I must let it go. You must let it go.
If we would just let it go, think of how much
more the Love of Christ would be spread
abroad in our lives. Think of how much more
His glory would fill our temple? We are all one
in the same body. This great glorious body that
He died to redeem. Love covers a multitude of
sins. He did it for me, will you allow Him to do
it for you?

ook into that Black face –

You Brown Eyes, You

Black Race

I realize that Almighty

God made you that way.

The shades of brown curly and straight

Did you know it was God's grace? That

protected you, kept you from your fears?

As I look and I see, the pain, the hurt, the anger

Am I really free?

What Is truth?   What is real?

Will I allow the enemy to steal?

Truth. Real. Freedom is Christ

Love, Hope Power not Strife.

In the Mirror what do I see? A man. A woman,

Black face – Jesus went to Calvary.

Don't you know? Don't you see? The shame

He can wash away?

Into the sea of forgetfulness He will throw

Your pain, sorrow, and chains.

But you my sister, you my brother, you my

mother, you my father

Must open the door and let Him in.

For how long will you carry these shackles and

chains that bind you?

If only you could open yourself, so that you

could truly find you.

The Vision

What man knows the plans you have for me? You have written them upon the pages of my heart, by your Spirit. Even some of the deep things, I do not know, because I could not perceive them. But you are faithful to complete the good work You have begun in me. Your purposes and plans for me will come forth like

You have ordained them to be. You made me and called me by name. When I was in my mother's womb you knew me and knit me together. You have accepted and justified me through the adoption of your Son. You have made me an heir and joint heir with Him. Your plans for me are great, who could fathom?

The turmoil, despair and rejection that once were my companions are no more. Because of You they have no place in my life. You replaced them with peace, joy, love and acceptance. Instead of loneliness I have fellowship with You. You gave me beauty for ashes. The ashes of my broken, torn and tattered life. The beauty of the Love of Christ. The beauty of grace and compassion. A healing salve for my wounded heart. You gave me the oil of joy for mourning. Mourning for things I wish I had but did not get.. The oil of joy to fill the empty places in my heart. The garment of praise for the spirit of heaviness. You gave me a song to sing, a new song. A song of the Spirit to replace a downcast countenance. Thanksgiving and praise as a garment and a cloak. You made me to be like a tree of righteousness, planted by the Living Water, with roots that go down deep, so that You can be glorified. Be glorified in the fruit that my branches bear, and the flowers that bloom. Be glorified by the seeds that I drop into fresh soil, as they reproduce after their own kind. You continue to rain down showers from heaven, fresh water for my branches to drink. And the Glory of your Son, and presence gives me light to live. Because I am firmly attached and grafted into your vine, and that is the only way that I can bear fruit – For Apart from You I Can Do Nothing.

What Is Going On?

rother is

rising

against

brother and

sister against sister. Mothers are turning their

backs on children and fathers are gone. Pastor

said, "Beloved, These are perilous times".

When will we recognize and see the strategy of

the enemy. He's trying to sift you like wheat. If

he could only get you to turn away from God,

the only real solution to every problem. If he could only get you involved in the system. He tries to tempt you. Quick money! Quick money! The dope block, the crack dealer, the gang banger and the beat slanger. Lookin for love in all the wrong places.

The policeman. The Jail House. Welfare and Poverty. History Seems to repeat itself. The enemy will try by any means necessary to ensnare you. He ensnared your ancestors in Chains then. And he will try to enslave you in

Chains now. Chains in your mind. Chains in your emotions. Chained to a drug. Chained to an inmate number. Chained to a lifestyle. Chained to a relationship.

The enemy will try by any means necessary to ensnare you.

Don't you see him? He's trying to make you hate the other man, the one who looks different from you. The one who talks different and worships different. Distrust, resentment, and blame breed hatred.

Why can't we all just get along?

\\\\\\\\\\\\\\\\\\\\\\\\\\\\\\\\\\\\\\

In the last days men will be lovers of themselves. Lovers of money. Daughter will rise up against mother and son against father. Making a lie out to be the truth and the truth to be a lie.

But we have this Blessed hope…

In the last days I will pour out my Spirit upon all flesh. All flesh! White flesh. Black flesh. Yellow flesh. Red Flesh. The Spirit of God will be poured out. And His Glory shall be manifested to all nations!

In response to the question, What's Going On?

\\

We are in the midst of the greatest battle in history. Not a fight between white and black with fists and sticks, but a spiritual war against the enemy who operates behind the scenes. The weapons of our warfare are not carnal, but they are mighty through God to the pulling down of strongholds.

Take up your weapons of war and prepare for battle mighty warrior. God's gonna pour His Glory out on you and make you an instrument in His hand. There is no time to become distracted by the subtle messages of division between black and white.

There are too many people waiting on you.

Waiting for you to accept His call and walk in

His power.

What's Going On? Now you know. What are

you gonna do about it?

Jesus Cheerleader

esus Cheerleader! For this I was created. Regardless of my age, Man or woman; Child or babe, You are on the stage – As a Jesus Cheerleader.

Little girl you thought poms poms and a loud voice was all there was; Flips and cartwheels and standing straight and standing tall; but only to help you see what a real Cheerleader is supposed to be; You are a Jesus Cheerleader the highest call, bringing praises and a shout to your God.

Celebrate! Raise the Praise. Clap your hands, Shabach! Crazy Praise. Slapping the enemy. Cymbals, Drum Beats, Chords and Harmonies; The Jesus Cheerleader has songs to sing. Inhale. Exhale. Let everything that has breath praise the Lord! Let everything that has breath praise the Lord! Let everything that has breath praise the Lord! Syncopation, the Blink of my eyes; Every breath with the rise and fall of my chest. I hear sounds; Instruments. An orchestra inside my head. My heart beat, pulsating blood, every cell, muscles and fibers; Motions and rotations; Systems and Functions. Even my breath is a Jesus Cheerleader. Oceans rise; the rush of the tide. The dust of the desert sand blows by. The flowers bloom awakening their smiles to the sunlit sky. Gras blades grow from seedlings stretch forth their eyes Even the Rocks Cry! The Rocks Cry! The Rocks Cry! Jesus Cheerleader!

Birds sing and the rain drops bow down, The baby cries aloud at birth. Ants march and the

Mantis prays; The trees dance and sway to the beat of the wind. Jesus Cheerleaders!

If I don't praise I won't make it to the place. If I don't praise I will fall down and stay.

Blessings not cursing; Raising not hurting. Created for this purpose.

Jesus Cheerleader is a warrior; Skillful in the battle. Because I choose to give up and give the fruit of my lips. I can never loose. Never loose. Never loose. My praise contains the atmosphere for change; I open my mouth and swords come out! Tears down the walls;

Destroys the chains and breaks down the gates.

I am a Jesus Cheerleader!

I am a Jesus Cheerleader to make him smile
and become the apple of His eye. His grace and
His pleasure shines on me; In my Praise He
lives and dines with me. Jesus Cheerleaders
you have to praise, because if you don't you
will forever ruin your days. It's never too late
to see the state of your Jesus Cheerleader
praise. It takes only a second to realize. Who
am I on the inside? You are a Jesus Cheerleader
with the power of the creator. When you open
your lips and give thanks from your heart;

Raise your hands and sing; Dance and clap,

Sway from side to side; The King of Glory

enters in.

Now that you know who you are, you are ready

for the greatest moments of your life.

Jesus Cheerleader.

\\

.

Mirror

Mirror, Mirror what do you see? Only the face staring back at me.

God made you expressly by his hand

Why is it so hard for you to understand?

What makes up that face Brown Eyes?

Character, Strength, Beauty and Style

Identity

It's not In the eye of the beholder, But identity
is really the Christ that set me free. He made
me new, made me clean, over again.

I am redeemed! Now I see that the Greater One
is Inside Me

So once again I ask, What do you see?

The real truth? His Glory, Fruit, The Word and
His Authority

Believe it, It's true – Whoever would have
thought?

The person staring in the mirror is you?

Many troubles, trials and disappointments you have gone through. But these He has used to make mold and shape you

So when you look into that mirror what do you really see?

I can finally look and see, I accept and believe, It's Me.

The Day I Met You

he Day I met you, I
was surprised.

We sang together.

Surprised my heart responded.

Surprised you cared so much about me and
called me friend.

If It had not been for Pearl and Elton,
the day I met you would have never been.

\\\

If it had not been for the first failing to realize the gift she had, the day I met you would have never been.

If I had completely unraveled when the enemy threw his best shot at me, the day I met you would have never been.

The day I met you was the opportunity for you to be to me, and me to be to you exactly what we both prayed for ; It was our chance to show unconditional love, non- judgmental friendship and sacrifice.

The day I met you was the opening paragraph in a new volume of works written as a tribute to a new start.

The day I met you was the foundation beneath the building blocks of purpose, future and greatness; You and I together.

The day I met you was the opening song in a lifetime concert of classical music and loves sweet melodies; Me and you.

I am so glad you were born so that I could celebrate and remember the day I met you;

Happy Birthday - With Love, Brown Eyes

Love Degrees

ove is the foundation for all things. Love is pure. It is strong and covers all. Love's cornerstone is Christ's enduring love for me; That He died for me. I wanted to reach for you, but I had to accept God's Love first. Then I thought I was ready, but I was divided within secretly. Attachments and confusion were All over my mind. But then I came to see myself as I was;

Truly loving the reflection for the first time. The smooth places and peaceful faces, the many aspects of who I am. I became one with Christ, and then I was totally One on the inside. The outward and the inward came together in Unity. I Welcome you to every part of the real me. The lover of my youth and my ageless days, You deserve to have me complete and altogether. No fragments or broken pieces, No baggage or fake exterior, but the restoration of love allows my heart reception to the precious gift. Love is parallel, vertical, horizontal, symbolic and tangible. It is Truth. Love is so great that it calls out my name in the silence;

Love is the warm embrace of His Words to me.

Jesus is the first Lover of my soul. He taught

me how. I am ready to love you, because I am

loved and I love myself. The Two shall become

one flesh, and like a Cord of Three Strands that

is not easily broken, Love shall tightly wrap us

together. Love can never fail. To be one with

you; I must first be one with me. I am ready.

One love that is never ending, constantly

enduring, always covering, forever giving, at

all times serving, continually forgiving; Daily

growing, living, and increasing. In the beauty

of this Love, I am One. You are One. Together

We are One.

Unlocked Potential

am God's Masterpiece. Fearfully and wonderfully made to bring forth. Daughter is who He calls Me, I am made in His image,

Specifically and specially Designed; He loves me so much

\\\

He even gave me His mind. I think about

things that are

Lovely, pure, and of a good report. My mind is

sound and

Renewed daily; Washed and transformed by

God's Words.

My imagination is a creative canvas for the

expressed purpose

and potential of God. I can see what is unseen

through the eyes

of faith. Because I have the mind of Christ, My

Sight is Right;

With my eyes I see, with my heart I receive, with my mouth

I speak and with my feet I step into increase. The potential of

God in me is Released; The Power of God in me now Unleashed.

I Rise Up and Declare, Walk and Serve, Live and Give,

Teach and Lead; Called and Chosen to Fulfill Destiny. Faith

In action responds to God's gentle leading in my heart. My

Mouth Speaks what He says only, and

everything within me

Agrees. My words are the action steps that

build and carry

Out The Flow that has been Unlocked. This is

My year, This is My time, My due season for

Prosperity, Spirit, Body and Mind.

Personal Process

I am an anointed woman of God. An oracle of God. His Mouthpiece. I flow and function in the prophetic ministry. God gives me words to write. I am a woman who was broken and wounded. The devil attempted to ruin me and make my days dark. But God had plans to prosper me and heal my wounded heart. He has blessed my mind and my hands to write. He will bring my gifts before great men and elevate me to new heights. I am learning how to flow and function in what God has given me. There is only one, never to be repeated or seen again. Leigh Karen. When God made me he broke the mold. Today I celebrate Jesus in me. Today I appreciate myself. I acknowledge the gifts He's stored in me and to God's Spirit I yield and say yes. In my yielding His greatness will be released. In my surrendering - His Glory shown. Opening doors no man can close. Maximize the moment, maximize my space .Promotion is coming,

Deeper Depths, A Higher Place.

Go Through

You are my peace in the middle of the storm. My help in time of trouble. My way when there is no way. My friend when I am lonely. My mother and father when I am rejected or neglected. My pain You bore. Healed my wounds; In your stripes there is healing; Physical and emotional.

You took on the chastisement of my peace. You bore my pain, You carried my sorrows and were acquainted with My grief. The pain is real, yet You are my way through. I am hid In You, and You live in me. How can a mother remember one daughter, yet forget the other? But your love reaches even the shores of the lonely heart, longing for things to be different. Seeking understanding for a father who doesn't remember his only child; Always hoping for a phone call. Making excuses; Always accepting; In the Midst of their rejection.

\\\

Love is a two way street? Maybe many more ways it seems. Many dimensions to love; Not what it says but what it does. I love, even though there is a struggle to show the love their lips decide.

A defining Moment. Aha! Realizing I have received a gift greater than any ever bought. The Love of God: So multidimensional, multifaceted; Reaches into my heart where untouched and quiet places reside.

Defining moment. Today I realize I am who I am precisely because of my mother and father giving me life. Years later stories to tell.

Histories and mysteries reveal the Truth; God's

Love overcomes All evil still. A counselor to

the hurt, broken and bent over; How can I when

heart pain I have ? Because of Christ I live, yet

I would have been gone. Long ago Rescued; A

Purposeful love accepted me and called me it's

own.

Cold, closed, unattached, disconnected; Lonely,

alone, rejected. No more. It stops now. With

Me.

\\

I will love them despite handicaps; God's love the only remedy.

Now I understand why my life; Understand how it is. Because I had to see the greatest gift of all is Love wrapped up inside of me.

Open wide the gates, the doors to my heart, my mouth I will declare; The free gift of love for each person I pass so God they'll come to know.

Out of great adversity, struggle, pain and heartache comes a precious and costly thing; I know God you created me to love, to write, to counsel and to sing.

Thank you for keeping me, upholding me and preventing the unraveling of my mind. Thank you that I did not jump, thank you for touching me so I did not give up. Thank you for making me an example to help, thank you for peace in exchange for pain. You are my Lord and King, Heavenly Father I give You praise.

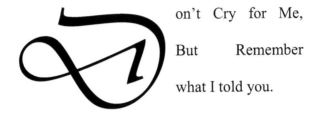on't Cry for Me, But Remember what I told you.

Never Forget the words I said as they were only meant to help you. Don't Cry for Me, But Remember What I Taught You. That there is always a lesson of "what if" so you'll be ready for tomorrow. Don't Cry for Me, But remember

What I Showed You. To take the time to help
someone in the small things that really matter
Don't Cry for Me, But Remember How I much
Love You and did everything I could to provide
for you and protect you. Don't Cry for Me, But
Remember How I Lived Life, and worked and
served so everyman could have opportunity.

Don't Cry for Me, But Remember I Laughed
and Lived Fully. So Practice This One Thing
That I Preached. Don't Cry For Me, But
Remember When You Are Ready To Listen,

My Lessons Are Always Here to Teach

In remembrance of

Melvin Laverne Davis August 5, 2006

Section Three - Soul Verse

Failure - Functioning - Perfection

ho defines success? Who defines failure?

What is failure anyway? Is it that a righteous man falls down seven times but he gets up again? Is it the falling down process? Is it that you actually fell? Is it how long you stayed down when you fell? Is it the fact that you got

\\\

up and just because you fell it doesn't matter even if you ever got up again? Who defines failure? Is it God's Word that says what failure is and what is success? Is it man and his ideology and his rules and his laws? God's Word or Man's expectation? Who defines failure? Do I define failure for myself? Do I allow others to construe for me what failure really is in my own life? Or is failure just a part of the process? Is failure a part of what it takes for me to learn and grow and develop and to change? Who defines failure?

Failure is Opportunity.

Turn it around! What it takes to change. An Orchestrated dance in the lifespan of the maturation cycle. A bump in the middle of my road toward the fulfillment of God's call and plan for me. A roadblock turned into a stepping stone to help me climb higher toward my destiny. A pothole in the pavement to prepare me for transition in all types of terrain. Failure is often what it will take to push me across the line. I'll make the choice to walk through the door from failure to purpose. In the end and looking back, the failings of my past will have all been a part of my future.

Functioning

Do you know you can be functioning and failing? You can be functioning but not feel like you fit. You can be functioning and feel left out. You can be functioning, but seeming as if no one even recognizes *where* you are. Feeling as though there's no value, feeling as though no one recognizes *why* you are, what you've done, even who you are. Seems like no one is listening? You can be functioning and people relate to you based on your function, not based upon who you are. You can be functioning, your value being tied up in what you can provide and what you can offer and what you can do, rather than the substance of what really makes up you. Rehearsed motion, functioning like you always do. Aren't you missing something? Machine like repetitious action. God made you too diverse and multidimensional to maintain such a limited existence. Function in the fullness of your capacity, and fulfill the call. Fulfill the call. Completely, leaving nothing, fulfill the call. Function and fit into your place in the body and then you will be connected to the parts that enable you to perform effectively.

Perfection

How can you dare to see yourself as not
needing what you proclaim? Some time with
the Father and a touch by the Master; After that
you'll never be the same. Never be the same.
Driven. You are not perfect. And never will be.
Give yourself a break. It's okay to make
mistakes. You have permission.

Sit down. Rest. And talk to the Physician.

 am a minister. A minister of the Gospel of the Reconciliation and Restoration of Jesus Christ. My message is that he restored and healed me, so therefore He can also restore and heal you. I am anointed. I am a Woman of Prayer. I am a sanctified, consecrated, Spirit filled woman, and I obey the Words of God. I am a praying woman and a

warring woman. I warfare in the spirit, by prayerful intercession. I hear God's voice, I operate in the prophetic ministry. I am His Daughter and His Friend, because that is what He calls me. I am His Beloved and I am in covenant relationship with Him. He is my First Husband. Nothing can destroy the bond between us. I am His workmanship, I am beautiful and wonderfully made. I am a masterpiece. I have unique gifts, talents, skills and abilities. I have been created to worship and praise. I have been created for relationship. I willfully go into worship. I love to worship and praise My God because of what He has done and who HE is to me.

My hearts desire is to serve God with every gift, every talent and every skill He has given me. If I sing, I will sing for Him. If I write and recite poetry, I will speak for Him. If I work, I will work for Him. If I counsel, I will counsel for Him. If I lead, I will lead for Him. When I relate, I will relate in Him. When I love, He will love through me. Any deficiency or weakness in me is filled and covered because of God in me.

He is the reason that I live and move and have my being. Without God, I am nothing. With God, I am everything, I can accomplish anything, and I am able to do all things. God is the well from which my life springs forth.

Therefore, I am blessed to be a blessing, and I walk in my wealthy place. I am blessed in every place I go, and everything that comes in contact with me is blessed. Abraham's blessings are mine, so I can never be broke another day in my life. I am a channel for the blessings and prosperity of God's Favor.

I am a Kingdomprenuer and a financier of the Gospel, and my increase shall be for the kingdom. God has blessed my house, because I have blessed His house. I am consumed by the zeal for the house of the Lord. His house shall be great – even the City of Restoration shall spring up and be a blessing to the harvest. I will always serve in the House of the Lord. Destiny, vision, purpose and God's call for me have met together on one road towards the City of Restoration. I will serve God in my community and be a living epistle for others to read. My life has been preparation for service in this place. I will work and serve God and not man, because God brings the increase. I do not seek after man's favor or praise, but my reward comes from the Man I serve. To every thing there is a season, and a time. Regardless of external influence and what I see, I will

faithfully serve and complete the work at my
hand.

Spirit to Spirit

he water of your

presence washes me

from within.

Removes all fear;

Saturates my soul.

I am lost in your Glory.

Nothing else matters.

Pressing in deeper: Pursuing You further.

Drawing closer, I worship thee.

Soul cracked open; Bared naked before you.

Flowing out of me now.

My desire for you.

    I want the water of Your presence to

    saturate my soul.

    Holy Spirit pour down till Glory

    overflows.

    Rain More, Rain More, Rain More.

When You Were Born

hen you were born, Heaven was at attention. The clouds laughed, the raindrops danced, the moon and the stars remembered, while the sun danced at the fashioning of God's Hands. For Sharon, the baby blessing.

Sweet baby Shay Shay, don't cry; God has given you the prophet's eye; Little girl learning now, it's okay, a double edged sword in your mouth God gave you, to preach and to pray;

Little Girl sing Praises! On the Instruments

Play! Anointed Gifts and Melodies in God's

presence you parade. God gave you His heart

to love a child whose parent's were gone; gave

you His mind to think only what His Word says

I am; gave you his eyes to see past the anger

into the suffering places; and gave you His

hand to reach me so I couldn't die with the

dream still alive.

It was too late after you came. The path was

already laid. Destruction was cancelled and

Ruin had been faltered. Rejection had been removed and the devil's plans were already halted. The Father's Love built a shelter for you and an Altar. His Word Transformed the Seedling into a Beautiful Flower. The mirror of God's Word let you see clearly. The Perfect Law of Liberty made you free completely.

50 now, time for celebration! Renewed and Increased Glory in you; Dumamis Power Habitation. You are the mouthpiece of God, Chosen for this hour. No limits, No Boundaries for you, Only Increase All Around. Love for

Sharon, Wife, Mommy, Sister, Auntie, God-Mother, and Co-Pastor. We Love you and Celebrate this season - your birthday with great expectation of God's coming glory and demonstration.

Written for Pastor Sharon Burns - Surprise Birthday Celebration August 18, 2007

\\\

Love

ove. Opened the door to my lost heart. Love. Closed the chapters of my past, gave me a new start. Love. Love. Love. Love.

Love gave music sweet melodies. Love gave inspired words to write.

Love saw my future, gave present to my past; A free gift, life's blessings at last.

Love made the end my beginning. Love established you plus me to be us and we.

3 Strands together. Love made.

Love Is. God. Love searched for me and knew

me when I didn't know.

Love called me by name. Love became what I

needed to hear and needed to be.

Love Rescued me.

Written by Leigh Karen Graves-Ware

and

Malvin C. Ware, Sr

Love Is...

 ove is special.

Love is kind. Love is yours.

Love is mine. Love is hot.

Love is fine.

I Love you Mom, All the time.

Written by Malvin C. Ware, Jr.

Tattoo

 aybe he thought

that if he endured pain for something that will last forever then his mother will forever be with them.

It is like giving back.

Because the mother endured pain to bring the person into the world and her love lasted forever. So, maybe the person felt that he was giving back what was given to him…

Written by Chloe Denai Ware

Strength

My name is Qadara, but I go by the alias of Truth when I write, because Truth is what I am always in search of, and hope to embody. This spoken word is called Strength, and it is dedicated to ALL my Sistas. This is not to discredit my brothers at all. So, if you're living right.....keep it up, stand strong and stand tall. But this one's for the ladies; here's a shout out for you. To acknowledge the awesome and amazing things that we do. I was sitting reflecting the other day, as I often do when it's quiet. And, I had a moment where I was thinking about how strong women of color had to be and continue to be. And I felt filled with adoration and pride for my sisters. Yes, we were all taught about the

\\

sisters of past, your Harriet Tubmans, your Ida B. Wells, your Correta Scott Kings, and so on. Strong powerful women of color! But even today, as the times continue to be hard We press on! The woman who carries her family on her back, Works 2 jobs, raises her children, teaches them morals. I applaud you! Many do this alone, and yet still so fabulous! The professional woman, who is handling business in the board room, running things, in spite of the many obstacles she had to overcome to get there. I applaud you! The woman who might not have made the best decisions for her life, but found her way out of the darkness. I applaud you! And to those who are still in the dark, slipping, falling, but still get up and continue to press forward. I applaud you! Yes we may slip, trip, and back slide, But as you brothers may attest, no one gets up more gracefully or consistently than a sista. So ladies, You keep being fabulous, you keep being fine, Beautiful, magnificent, sassy, divine! Stay strong! Stay encouraged! Stay classy! Stay smart! Use wisdom, intelligence, your mind and your heart! And I don't speak these words because I think that you need, Me to stroke your ego or have flattery to feed. I mean it through and through and am honored to stand amongst you. We carry heavy burdens, but still move with such grace And our smile, despite our pain, still can brighten a place Life comes through us, we give knowledge and love, Work hard, but find time to praise the All Mighty above So all that being said, don't forget that you're great! And a truly worthy cause, to feel proud and celebrate! Clap your hands! Stomp your feet! Do a dance! Walk it out! Cause today, you're the reason to get excited and shout! *I implore you to remember, When facing challenges of great length Love yourself through your struggles! Never disregard your Strength!*

Food for thought: A Woman's greatest flaw is the neglect of oneself. We are so busy, that in the midst of our giving to others, loving others, earning money, maintaining the health of those around us, we forget to give to ourselves what we offer to everyone else. So today, don't forget to love yourself. Peace and Blessings.

Written By Qadara Farih Moore, a.k.a. Truth

Introduction - About the Author

 Leigh Karen Graves-Ware was born in Southeastern Connecticut and raised in a family where education and service to community was stressed. Raised by her mother, father, grandparents, aunt and uncle, the proverb *"it takes a village to raise a child"* was made manifest in her life. Growing up, she had the opportunity to live and travel throughout the East Coast, West Coast, and the Southern states. This exposure to people of different cultures and communities presented challenges, and offered many opportunities. A multi-generational support system and personal determination to

succeed helped Leigh to respond to brokenness and loss. At the breaking point, she experienced a turning point coming face to face with the love and grace of God. In the pinnacle of crisis, she became acquainted with the Lord Jesus Christ and the healing began. It was then, that she came in contact with the restorer of the broken heart and came to live the words…

"(He) Gave me beauty for ashes, the oil of joy for mourning, the garment of praise for the spirit of heaviness, that they might be called trees of righteousness, the planting of the Lord, that He may be glorified" (Is 61:3 KJV)

Through adversity and life's challenges, she learned the power of the written word as a means of release and healing. The words that brought relief became an avenue for help and inspiration to others. Leigh functions in many aspects of ministry and has shared professionally as a poet, guest presenter, trainer, and speaker for workshops, retreats and special events. Leigh is employed as a supervisor in the criminal justice system and has served as a trainer in Spirituality, Substance Abuse, Women's Issues, Leadership and Development. Leigh has served in music ministry with her husband for over 17 years singing with the New Life Praise and Worship Team and The New Life Restoration Choir. She is a featured soloist and songwriter on the debut recording "Restore Me" and a founding Board Member of the Tzedaka Community Development Corporation. She works with Athletic Teams in her local community, and remains an active supporter of her children as student athletes. Leigh has successfully completed the Doctor of Ministry, Master of Social Work, and a Bachelor of Arts in Sociology. She also holds a license and certifications in substance abuse and co-occurring mental health and substance abuse. She is preparing to pursue her lifelong dream of law school, and finalizing the Ph.D portion of her ministerial training in Biblical Counseling. When asked to identify her greatest success, Leigh shared "my greatest accomplishment and the pinnacle of my life is being a mom and a wife". Leigh's personal mission is "to inspire and be inspired".

Made in the USA
Charleston, SC
30 November 2009